CHONDA PIERCE

A **BIBLE STUDY** ON THE **BOOK OF JOB**

LAUGHING
IN
THE DARK

FOR **WOMEN'S SMALL GROUP** OR **PERSONAL STUDY**

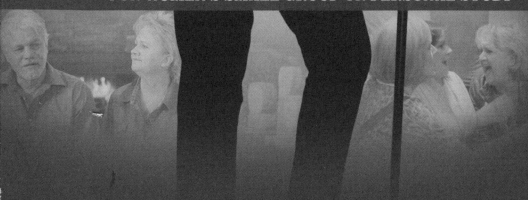

BY **CHONDA PIERCE** AND **DALE MCCLESKEY**

Dedication

It is always easy to stand proudly and give God the Glory for all the accolades or good days that come your way. The difficult time to say, "I give God all the Glory," is when we feel bruised and battered, crawling our way to the podium! But I can truly say, I give God ALL the glory for everything. Without Him, I would be nothing nor would I have survived this journey.

I dedicate this book and study to my son. We have crawled through some of the most difficult days of our lives - together. May you see God alive and working in ALL things, Zach.

Chonda Pierce, 2016

Contents

Chonda Pierce

Armed with an abundance of unpretentious Southern charm and laser sharp wit, Chonda Pierce has been entertaining audiences from coast to coast for more than 20 years. An in-demand stand-up comic, television hostess and author, Pierce has parlayed her gift for storytelling into a multi-faceted career.

Pierce has authored eight books, has ranked among Pollstar's top-selling live performers and received an award from the RIAA as the bestselling female comedian in history.

She's a frequent guest on the famed Grand Ole Opry and has served as host of the Inspirational Country Music Awards and Christian Music Hall of Fame Awards as well as co-hosting the GMA Dove awards. She received FIVE Daytime Emmy nominations for her work co-hosting "Aspiring Women" and her first television special, "This Ain't Prettyville!" appeared on CMT (Country Music Television) nationwide. She has appeared on Life Today, The Wanda Sykes Show, The Mike Huckabee Show, as well as ABC's popular talk show, the View.

Dale McCleskey

Dale is a semi-retired pastor, writer, and editor. For the 24 years he worked as women's ministry editor at LifeWay Christian Resources. He always wanted to work with Chonda, so sharing in this study has been both a labor of love and joy. He lives in Mt. Juliet, Tennessee with his wife Cheryl and several thousand honeybees.

Introduction

Thank you for picking up and hopefully for participating in this Bible study. While making Laughing in the Dark, we talked about the need for a follow-up. We knew the story would resonate with many women, and that it would stir some difficult emotions. We wanted to create an opportunity to talk about and process the thoughts and emotions prompted by the movie.

I believe the Bible answers the deepest needs of our hearts. We began to pray about a Bible study subject that would do several things:
- Help women turn to God's Word for answers;
- Provide an opportunity for God's people to support each other in the struggles of life;
- Provide a safe place to share the emotions exposed by the movie;
- Create an opportunity for Christians and churches to reach out to their communities.

Then we realized, the Book of Job speaks to every one of those concerns. We decided it would make a good study for what God had placed on our hearts.

We've tried to keep the group time process simple and practical. We suggest a small group of women meet for six weeks.

The first week the group will watch the movie together and spend a few minutes getting to know each other. Then during the following week, complete the personal Bible study from the Book of Job. Take time to write your responses in the study. You'll be amazed how God can use your pen and paper to bring wisdom and understanding in your life. While I cannot be physically present, we've prepared the study with the questions I'd ask if I could personally meet with you. Each week, the group will discuss topics from both the movie and the Job study.

Whether you're new to Bible study or you like to read the original Hebrew text for relaxation, I hope you will come to value Job like a dear friend. Though we cannot answer all the questions Job's story raises, I think we can learn a great deal from his experience. His story touches all of us, because all people suffer in ways we cannot explain.

So thank you and welcome to the study of Job. If you don't already have access to a group, why not start one? All you really have to do is invite some friends to watch Laughing in the Dark, and go from there. You'll find suggestions for starting and leading a group in the back of this book.

Week 1: Group Time
Getting Started

Welcome to Laughing in the Dark and the study of the Book of Job. I hope you can gather with some girlfriends to share the movie and study together. I hope you'll laugh together, cry together, and find strength to face life together. I also hope that the ancient patriarch named Job will become a personal friend. You'll see that you share much more in common with him than you might think. I hope Job will become a welcome addition to your group.

The first week we'll share the movie together. Look to the suggested leader helps in the back for some suggestions for conducting an effective group. Then do the Bible study in preparation for week 2.

Each week you'll watch some short clips from the movie. You'll find these on the Laughing in the Dark DVD in the special features section. Discuss the topic for the week, and discuss some of what God has been showing you through your personal study. Each week you'll have material on the topics raised by the movie and on the experience of Job. The suggested schedule looks like this:

Week 1: Movie and getting to know each other
Week 2: Loss
Week 3: Grief
Week 4: Doubt
Week 5: Truth
Week 6: Grace
Week 7: Optional review of week 6 and celebration

After the first week we suggest the following plan for group sessions:

1. Welcome and opening prayer
2. Watch the video clip(s) from the Laughing in the Dark DVD
3. Discuss the topic of the week, choosing from suggested questions
4. Review the print study from the previous week, choosing from suggested questions
5. Closing time of prayer

We've designed the suggested plan to provide flexibility for the needs of your group. Consider sharing leadership for the group time. Remember that you don't need to answer every question. You'll have a successful group if members have a safe and loving place to share their journey and study Job together.

At the end of your time together, consider having a time of celebration. A shared meal is always a great way to celebrate. You may even wish to eat together each week. (Of course, chocolate must be involved!) Be creative but keep it simple. Please don't create stress for yourself. I'm praying for you and with you. Enjoy your time of fellowship and study.

Now let's get started.

Movie

Watch the full movie, *Laughing in the Dark*, together.

From what you know of Job, what similarities do you see between the life of Job and Chonda's life?

What events in Chonda's life do you find similar to your own?

What do you hope to give and receive from this group study?

On To Personal Study

I hope that watching the movie has been encouraging. One of the ways Satan beats us up is with the feeling that we're alone. He tries to convince us we're unique in negative ways. Uniquely broken. Uniquely wrong. Uniquely alone. Isolated. I hope sharing my brokenness has made it easier to share yours.

When we face our hurts, we also need to know where to turn with them. Scripture speaks to our needs at so many levels. As a follow-up to the movie, we're looking at the Book of Job. He was a man who knew suffering. However, we want to view Job in a different light. I suspect we usually think of Job as being very different than ourselves. We imagine him as so different that we can only stand back and admire him.

For these weeks we want to look at how very similar we are to Job. We will see many points we share. Some of them are good traits. Some are not. My hope is that together we will not simply learn facts; we will share a life journey with the ancient patriarch, with joys, sorrows, affirmation, and correction.

Do your Bible study this week, but please don't make it a chore. Enjoy your time with Job. You might even find his story makes you less alone in your journey.

Week 1: Personal Bible Study
Behind the Scenes: Job 1:1-11

In my first thoughts about Job I laughed at two huge contrasts. First I thought how God allowed Satan to go after Job because he was so pure and wonderful. That made me think, Well, if anyone compares me to Job, they've got the wrong girl. I am not a noble, perfect, Christian.

My second thought about Job involved his parenting. The book told how he sacrificed for his children. His children would have parties and just live life. Meanwhile daddy Job would go make a sacrifice and repent for them. He even offered sacrifices for sins they might have committed. Suddenly I realized Job was among the worst parents on the planet! He never let his kids suffer their own consequences. And that's when it hit me: Now Job, that's where I'm exactly like you. You are a brother from another mother!

When I realized Job had a black belt in enabling, I thought, Oh my, that doesn't make me feel so bad about myself now. Because man, was I ever—and still am—the classic enabler. I'm not as bad as I used to be, but I still struggle with that. (If you're like me, go find and insert the name of a good counselor here!)

Had you ever noticed that? Job was a great man, of both great integrity and great wealth. Those things serve to distance us from Job. This same man was certainly not so great a parent. I'd like to suggest that all these things invite us to identify with him.

If you come to this study with some knowledge of the Book of Job, how do you generally feel about him?

Do you think of Job as being like you? Why or why not?

Many Bible scholars believe Job came from the time of Abraham or before. If so, Job lived in the world that remembered God created the world but that had none of the revealed truth of Scripture. Their theology basically boiled down to punishment and reward. They thought God gave good people good things and punished bad people.

In the Book of Job we find a previously wealthy, successful, and good man who became beset with enormous problems. In our lives, we all find ourselves facing problems as well. I'm just guessing none of us are as wealthy as Job, nor do we possess greater personal integrity. But we all at least want to be known as good people. We want to be better people than we are, even if our history shows we've failed in all sorts of ways.

Likewise we all share at least a desire to have financial security. We probably don't own several thousand camels (Thank goodness for that! Did you ever smell a camel?), but we'd sure like to have enough in the bank that we don't have to worry about the monthly bills. So we can automatically identify with Job in several ways.

Would you rather have financial security or the respect of people in your community? Why?

What do you think it would require for you to be considered a "person of perfect integrity who turned away from evil"?

How can a person have both integrity and also fall short of the glory of God?

Romans 3:23-24 says "all have sinned and fall short of the glory of God. They are justified freely by His grace through the redemption that is in Christ Jesus." Of course Job lived long before Jesus came, so we have an advantage here.

How does the last part of the Romans passage indicate an imperfect human being can have fellowship with a Holy God?

- ○ By attending church every week;
- ○ By being honest in their business dealings;
- ○ By grace through the redemption that came by Christ;
- ○ By only telling an occasional white lie.

Yes, God loves and accepts us based on Jesus and His sacrifice. Do you think you'd rather have Job's perfect integrity or forgiveness of sins through Jesus? Why?

Think of what the New Testament said about John the Baptist. When Jesus began His ministry, John was the most renowned holy man alive. But Jesus said, "I tell you, among those born of women no one is greater than John, but the least in the kingdom of God is greater than he" (Luke 7:28).

What do you think the phrase, "the least in the kingdom of God is greater" (than John the Baptist) means?

Job was a fallen human being, just like you and me. The best of Job's integrity was still tainted by sin. I think that means anyone forgiven by Christ's redeeming blood is more righteous than John the Baptist or Job could be, even on their best day.

The question is, would you rather be Job, with his personal righteousness, or a sinner saved by grace? I think a lot of people would really rather be good enough on their own so they didn't have to depend on Jesus. As we read Job's story, I think it's fair to ask if he was one of those people. Was Job really more committed to God or to his own goodness?

If you are acquainted with the story of Job, you know what happens next. Satan went into the presence of God. God seemed to taunt Satan with Job's faithfulness (Job 1:8). Job's human faithfulness showed just how unfaithful Satan had been. God seemed to be saying, that while Satan had once known all the benefits of fellowship with God, he still rebelled. But Job, though a member of the fallen human race, was far more faithful.

Would you see the situation differently if you pictured God not taunting Satan, but rather speaking with grief and concern, saying, "Satan, I loved you but you betrayed Me. See how Job remains faithful though knowing Me so much less." How would such a thought impact your view of God?

Satan determined to remove this reminder of his own guilt. Thus was born the story of Job. Satan went to God with a most peculiar charge and request.

> *"Satan answered the LORD, 'Does Job fear God for nothing? Haven't You placed a hedge around him, his household, and everything he owns? You have blessed the work of his hands, and his possessions have increased in the land. But stretch out Your hand and strike everything he owns, and he will surely curse You to Your face'" (Job 1:9-11).*

What did Satan suggest as the basis for Job's integrity (Job 1:9-10)?

What did Satan think would quickly destroy Job's faithfulness (Job 1:11)?

What do you think would be the outcome of a world where faithfulness to God was always rewarded and unfaithfulness was promptly punished?

Can you imagine a world where human freedom and creativity would be replaced by punishment and reward? If every time we disobeyed we were immediately punished, would we mature to be wise adults? What would result if we reared children with a shock collar that hit them every time they did or thought the least thing wrong? Would you want to live in such a world?

I fear the result would be loveless and dark. We'd all learn to obey but out of programming and fear. Maybe God really does know best even in allowing humans such outlandish displays of freedom—even the freedom to flaunt God Himself.

You've probably never thought Job's story was your story, but it may surprise you. Consider each of the following aspects of the intro to the Book of Job in chapter 1.

Mark each statement either true or false.

____ **Job was a person of character and yet a fallen human being (vv. 1-3).**

____ **Job worked diligently to maintain his and his family's righteousness before God (vv. 4-5a).**

____ **Job lived in fear that his children would sin (v. 5:b).**

____ **Satan set out to destroy Job's favorable standing with God (v. 11).**

All of the statements above are true of Job. Do you think they may also apply in some sense to you and me as well? Have we attempted to be people of character, even though we have less than great success in the effort?

I suspect even the most twisted forms of parenting contain at least an element of desire that our families succeed. Have you, like Job, felt pulled between trusting God and fearing that we or those we love will run afoul of Him? And most of all, hasn't Satan, the enemy, set out to destroy us all (see 1 Peter 5:8)?

Next we see the beginning of a great cascade of calamities that Satan visits on Job and his family. First Satan attacked their possessions. When that failed he attacked Job's children. When Job still refused to accept defeat, Satan even turned to Job's health. Bit by bit Job descended into a pit of suffering. His losses would keep piling up until we find him in abject misery.

Loss

Loss is the universal human experience. As we progress through the stages of life, loss will accompany us at every step.

How would you describe the losses that come to every person in the course of a lifetime? List the normal forms of grief everyone must bear as they progress though life. I've given some answers for childhood as an example.

What losses occur in childhood?

We lose the comfort of having an adult care for our every need. Then we lose the sense that we are the center of the universe. We lose our innocence. We lose the ability to always get our own way. We lose the ability to trust some of the people around us. We discover that the world is a harsh place.

What losses accompany the teen years?

What do we lose in young adulthood?

What doors close to us in our middle years?

What do we gradually or suddenly lose as older adults?

In your life, which stage has contained the most severe losses so far?

Life can be described as a multiplying series of losses. We lose our innocence. We lose friends. At some point we lose our parents and the security they try to provide. We have to take responsibility for ourselves. With each decision or action, the window of opportunities closes a bit more. Ultimately we lose our youth, our heath, our loved ones, and finally life itself.

If this brings on feelings of depression, hang in there. We'll get back to hope and purpose soon.

While the losses we'll see in Job's life are compressed and dramatic, they bear a distinct resemblance to what you and I have or will face. So maybe we can identify with Job and his struggles in a more personal way than previously believed. In recovery groups they have a saying about not comparing your insides to other peoples' outsides. Maybe rather than letting Job's apparent integrity separate him from us, we ought to let his humanness draw him to us.

How do you identify with Job at each of the following points? Journal your thoughts to the statements below.

1. Like Job, I've tried to be a person of integrity.

2. Like Job, my fear of failure has sometimes caused me to become more self-centered and less God-centered.

3. Like Job, I've encountered situations that have baffled me and challenged my trust in God and His goodness.

4. Like Job, I've tried to control circumstances and people—especially my family.

Speaking of control, have you noticed yet that Job was a raging codependent? He wouldn't allow his children be responsible for themselves. He covered not only for what he knew they'd done, but he even offered sacrifices for what he thought they might have done. As the Book of Job progresses, watch for other ways he tried to maintain control of his circumstances and reputation.

Suffering

Suffering in this life is mandatory. If we compare the experience of people around us, it seems one person's life may look charmed while another may be inundated by troubles. But from the inside we'd see that every person suffers. From the time your life began in your mother's womb until you take your final breath one thing is certain: you and I will suffer. Job 5:7 says it this way, "mankind is born for trouble as surely as sparks fly upward."

We may buy into the false notion that God will spare us suffering. What do the following Scriptures say about that idea?

In Matthew 5:45 Jesus said "your Father in heaven ... causes His sun to rise on the evil and the good, and sends rain on the righteous and the unrighteous." What does that suggest about how God relates to all people?

What does the parable of the wheat and the weeds (Matthew 13:24-30) tell you about how God tends to deal with both good and evil?

How would the parable apply to good and evil in our lives as well as in the external world?

If the farmer pulled up the young weeds, he'd kill the wheat in the process. Maybe Jesus was suggesting that we are like the field. If God reached in and pulled up the evil in us—and heaven knows I've asked Him to enough times—He would destroy not just the evil but us in the process.

Whenever we pick up God's Word, we need to do a couple of things. One is to pray and ask God's Holy Spirit to open our eyes. He is the Author after all. The second thing is we need to identify with the characters. How are we like them? What can we learn from their experiences? In the first chapter of Job, we can come to several conclusions.

Conclusions

First we can connect to Job in our flawed efforts to be righteous. Even the worst of us have those moments when God might point to us with pride. Even the best of us have plenty of moments we'd like to hide.

Second, we all face the same enemy. Satan's very name means the accuser. Since the moment he tempted our oldest ancestors to try to become God for themselves, Satan has been accusing away. He tries his best to talk us into flaunting God's will. Then when we do, he promptly tells us we're no good because we listened.

Most of all we can guarantee suffering ahead. I certainly pray that my suffering and yours will not take the form of Job's losses. He lost his wealth, then his loved ones, and then his health. We're getting a little too far out over our skis here, but he'll lose everything except his unhelpful wife before our story really even gets started.

We can't predict what form our losses may take, but we've all got 'em. So the resolution we will see in the Book of Job certainly won't take the form of trouble-free living. But while suffering in this life is mandatory, doing it alone is not. We'll see that for Job and for us, losses can be eclipsed by an "absolutely incomparable eternal weight of glory" (2 Corinthians 4:17).

Review and Reflection

Are you better at feeling God's pleasure or His judgment? Explain.

Do you think those feelings tell you more about God or more about you? Why?

What truths or challenges do you take away from the start of Job so far?

Notes

Week 2: Group Time

Loss

The discussion topic for this week is the universal human experience of loss. The Bible study discussion comes from Job 1:1-11.

Suggested Opening Prayer: Heavenly Father, we know we live in a fallen world where every person experiences pain and loss. Thank You for entering our world and sharing our hurts and losses. We rejoice in Hebrews 2:9, "we do see Jesus—made lower than the angels for a short time so that by God's grace He might taste death for everyone—crowned with glory and honor because of His suffering in death." We know that since You tasted death for everyone, You alone can fully understand our hurts, just as You alone will ultimately deliver Your children from them. Guide us as we study, share, and pray together. We ask in Jesus' name, amen.

Movie Clip
As a group, watch the Bible Study-Week 2 video clips from the Laughing In The Dark DVD. You will find them on the special features section of the disc.

Video Discussion Questions

In what way or ways do you relate to Chonda's family, childhood, and losses?

What loss affected you most in your childhood or teen years?

How has loss impacted your relationship to God?

How do you think loss has impacted the way you relate to others?

Bible Study Discussion Questions ———

Page through your responses to the Bible study for week 1.

What one thing most stood out to you this week?

How do you think someone can be both a person of great integrity while also having areas of massive failure, like Job and his parenting?

As you came to this study, how did you generally view Job? Did you see him as like or unlike you? Why?

What do you think would be the outcome of a world where faithfulness to God was always rewarded and unfaithfulness promptly punished?

How would you describe the normal losses that come in life as we pass through life's stages?

So far, which stage of life has held the most difficult losses for you?

How does the biblical principles of "rain on the righteous and the unrighteous" (Matthew 5:45) and the parable of the wheat and the weeds (Matthew 13:24-30) help you relate to suffering?

Notes

Week 2: Personal Bible Study
The Beginning of Sorrows: Job 1:12-22

In the 19th century, during the early years of the China missions movement, famine frequently struck the land. Christian efforts to both spread the Gospel of Jesus and care for those suffering led to the term rice Christians. The term came about because starving people came for the rice rather than the Savior. It has come to mean anyone who seeks the benefits of Jesus without desiring the relationship with Jesus.

Have you observed people outwardly identifying with God or the Church seemingly without the inner reality? Have you seen people coming for what they can get out of Jesus rather than to worship Him?

Without naming names, what general kinds of examples could you cite?

What does Satan assert that God has placed around Job (Job 1:10)?

Have you noticed some people go to church to improve their business contacts? How about politicians who show up at churches before an election? The Book of Job begins with Satan's claim that Job was a "rice worshipper." Satan charged that Job only obeyed God because of the temporal benefits he got from serving Yahweh. So God granted Satan a stunning opportunity. He would get to torment Job to test whether his service came from love or self-interest.

Notice that the Book of Job presents a dual reality. God simultaneously protected Job and allowed holes to be torn in that protection. That may not be as different from you and me as we think.

If you were arguing the case that God had placed a hedge of protection around you, what evidence would you present?

What evidence suggests that God has allowed gaps in your hedge of protection?

Our reading of Job often distances him from us. We think how different he was. But in this portion of the Book of Job we begin to see our connection to him in a way none of us desire: Job suffers in ways that seem mindless and unfair.

What mind-boggling permission did God grant Satan in Job 1:12?

Remember that Job served as neither the writer nor narrator of the book. Nothing in the story indicates that Job ever knew about the conversation between God and Satan. Thus the calamities to come were complicated because they seemed to make no sense.

Think about a painful part of your life experience. How does the inability to determine the source or blame for suffering complicate your ability to deal with hurts?

Does this similarity in your experiences cause you to feel differently about Job? If so, how?

We identify with aspects of Job's story, but we need to recognize something else about him. Job's story is unique. Sometimes it's dangerous to make doctrines from stories. Stories in the Bible often illustrate what other passages teach. But do not confuse an event with a doctrine. The Bible absolutely teaches that God is both good and sovereign; it never teaches that God makes a regular practice of allowing Satan to ruin your life.

If you had to boil everything you know about the Book of Job down to a single teaching, what would it be?

If you are struggling with this question, look at an event from the Book of Luke.

At that time, some people came and reported to Him [Jesus] about the Galileans whose blood Pilate had mixed with their sacrifices. And He responded to them, "Do you think that these Galileans were more sinful than all Galileans because they suffered these things? No, I tell you; but unless you repent, you will all perish as well! Or those 18 that the tower in Siloam fell on and killed—do you think they were more sinful than all the people who live in Jerusalem? No, I tell you; but unless you repent, you will all perish as well!" (Luke 13:1-5).

Why did the people Jesus was addressing think bad things happen to people?

- ◯ Because we live in a sinful world and all deserve punishment.
- ◯ Because they had sinned and God was punishing them.
- ◯ Because God is just random and was toying with them.
- ◯ Because some people just naturally tick God off.

How do Luke 13 and the Book of Job address the same idea?

The Book of Job teaches very specifically that the common notion about evil and suffering is incorrect. Jesus addressed the same issue in Luke 13. Both Jesus and the Book of Job show that bad things happen for much more complex reasons than simply blaming the victim. Jesus added the fact that since we are all sinners, we all deserve punishment.

You can summarize the rest of the Book of Job in two unequal parts. First come a series of calamities brought on by Satan and misunderstood by all the earthly characters in the drama. Then in the final chapters of the Book, God deals with Job directly to bring resolution. But even in the end Job would never learn the details of the suffering that came upon him.

The First Series of Calamities ─────────────

One day when Job's sons and daughters were eating and drinking wine in their oldest brother's house, a messenger came to Job and reported: "While the oxen were plowing and the donkeys grazing nearby, the Sabeans swooped down and took them away. They struck down the servants with the sword, and I alone have escaped to tell you!"

He was still speaking when another messenger came and reported: "A lightning storm struck from heaven. It burned up the sheep and the servants and devoured them, and I alone have escaped to tell you!"

That messenger was still speaking when yet another came and reported: "The Chaldeans formed three bands, made a raid on the camels, and took them away. They struck down the servants with the sword, and I alone have escaped to tell you!"

He was still speaking when another messenger came and reported: "Your sons and daughters were eating and drinking wine in their oldest brother's house. Suddenly a powerful wind swept in from the desert and struck the four corners of the house. It collapsed on the young people so that they died, and I alone have escaped to tell you!" (Job 1:13-19).

In Job 1:13-19, the first blows came against Job's sons and daughters. A series of attacks by enemies and natural calamities first destroyed their herds and servants. Next a storm killed the adult children themselves.

Something about this passage struck me as odd. These servants ran to him to say, "all your sheep have been burnt up, all your camels are dead, and I'm still here to tell you about it." Weren't they the shepherds who were supposed to be taking care of the sheep?

Four people showed up like that. They kept running to Job and saying, "everything's destroyed but I was the only one who survived to come tell you." I was the only one who survived to come tell you. I'm thinking what happened to those people? You know what I mean? I'd be getting rid of them. I don't want any more friends to show up and give me more bad news.

These servants remind me of the times in my life when I got the news of two significant deaths. For example, when my big sister, Charlotta, died I had a friend who heard it on the radio and called me to say, "I'm so sorry."

I said, "I haven't heard anything. What are you talking about?" And he had to tell me. From that point on, our relationship was really never the same. Nothing wrong with him, but I was 16 years old, and you just have that awkward notion, "you're the one that delivered really bad news." Later when my little sister, Cheralyn, died I remember having a similar reaction when I heard she was gone. My family and I were at the hospital. As we congregated outside her room, a woman I barely knew was overly insistent that we embrace. It led to a long awkward moment until I squirmed to get away and ran to my mother at the end of the hall.

One friend called such people "crepe hangers." You probably wouldn't relate to that if you're under 50 and not from the South, but people used to hang crepe on the door to show mourning. Crepe hangers are people who just love to traffic in other people's misery.

Why do you suppose people sometimes relish sharing other people's faults, blame, or misery?

How do you deal with such people?

So every time one of those individuals came running to Job to say this had happened and I'm the one to survive to tell you about it, I thought, I know those people. I know those people who come to give you the bad news.

I am not as blameless as Job in my relationships or in my life. Yet here is a place where I do relate to him. People gave me similar advice. I got teary-eyed just talking about how many people came to Job saying, "Man, you should just throw up your hands and quit." I cannot tell you how many times I've heard that. Maybe not in those exact words but in statements like, "You ought to just get off the road for a while," or "You ought to just keep the family secrets." "Don't let people know about your depression." "Keep your pain to yourself." "I wouldn't discuss this or that."

Even my own brother said to me after writing my first book, "I don't know why you want to write about it. Nobody's going to believe us. You need to put the past in the past and step away. Look, I don't tell our story. I don't know why you're telling our story." He has since found miraculous hope and healing from those days long ago of "stuffing it all in." So yes! I've heard those naysayers many times in my life.

How about you? How do you deal with the "helpful naysayers" in your life?

Don't try to compare your losses to Job's. There is no way we can rank our griefs. Every loss, just as every person's life, is unique. Every loss and every person's response is private and personal. But by any measure Job's initial loss is monumental. Those of us who are parents probably can't imagine a greater degree of devastation than losing our children.

How did Job respond to the news of his losses (Job 2:10)?

What do you think was particularly good, godly, or healthy about Job's response?

What would you suggest might have been lacking in Job's response to loss or that might have improved his ability to deal with it?

I hope you have undertaken this study because you desire a greater love for God and a deeper relationship with Him. Most of us are also moved to study Job because we too suffer hurts and losses we cannot understand. Beware of setting yourself up to compete with Job. That's never a good idea. Neither should we put him on a pedestal. We can rightly be amazed at Job's reaction and also begin to question it.

I'm impressed that Job showed a profound lack of entitlement. His statement that he came into the world naked and would leave the same way (Job 1:21) seems to say, "I don't have a basis to complain. All of life is a gift, and God has still been good to me." On the other hand, I don't think Job had a particularly healthy way of dealing with his grief. He seems to have internalized it as if to say, "I can deal with this alone." We might even wonder if Job was stiff-necked in his righteousness.

Contrast Job's reaction with Jeremiah, who declared his grief openly.

> *Woe to me because of my brokenness—*
> *I am severely wounded!*
> *I exclaimed, "This is my intense suffering,*
> *but I must bear it."*
> *My tent is destroyed;*
> *all my tent cords are snapped.*
> *My sons have departed from me and are no more" (Jeremiah 10:19-20a).*

If you read Jeremiah 12:1-4 you will even see that Jeremiah argued with God, though He lost the argument in spectacular fashion. I think Jeremiah's approach leads to better mental health and a healthier understanding of God. So as our protagonist faces his first calamities, we can both admire Job and learn from his deficiencies.

How would you grade yourself on appreciating your strengths while honestly facing your weaknesses?

If you make a mistake, do you suddenly feel like pond scum? If so, why do you think that is?

Do you tend more to overestimate your strengths or to overemphasize your weaknesses? How does that show up in you?

One of the toughest things that loss does is that it leaves an emptiness that's never filled. So often I isolate or shut that empty part away from everyone or anything. Of course I can say from a spiritual standpoint that God has filled every empty gap. He has enriched my life, but the truth is, I will never have a sister again. So I can't just say, "Oh, God is going to send you other sisters." No, He sends relationships that are good, but I will never have another big sister, Charlotta, in my" life—never. I will never have another little sister, Cheralyn, in my life. That's what loss does. But healing helps us leave spaces open for something new.

Our friend Job is on a journey of deep loss—the valley of the shadow. His life, like ours, will never be the same.

Review and Reflection

How do you personally deal with the idea that God allows evil to strike His children?

What have you seen in Job's reactions to adversity so far that makes you feel friendlier to him?

Of the characters you've met in the Book Job, who would you most like to take to lunch?

Which of the characters would you most like to shake 'till their teeth rattle?

Notes

Week 3: Group Time

Grief

The discussion topic for this week is grief; which is the process to deal with the pain we feel when we experience loss. The Bible study content comes from Job 2:1-10.

Suggested Opening Prayer: Heavenly Father, You share with us all the events of our lives. We thank You for being present and adding to our joys. We bow before You with our grief. Thank You for Your Holy Spirit, our Comforter who comes alongside and carries us when our burdens become too much for us to bear. Teach us, we pray, to lean on You at all times. Teach us to follow You when the path grows rough and steep. We thank You that when we reach the end of ourselves in our pain, we still find You there for us. Teach us this week to grieve well. Thank You for the hope we have in Christ.

Movie Clip

As a group, watch the Bible Study-Week 3 video clips from the Laughing In The Dark DVD. You will find them on the special features section of the disc.

Video Discussion Questions

Chonda shared about losing her mother and David. What have been the most difficult two losses you have experienced?

What has helped you most in dealing with grief?

What has been the most helpful thing others have done for you in a time of grief?

What has been least helpful?

Chonda spoke of David's memorial as to a life well lived, yet David struggled with addiction. Job was a man of great integrity, yet one could certainly question his parenting. How do you think someone can be both a great person and a dismal failure at the same time?

How does it change our grieving process to admit both the good and bad in our loved ones?

Bible Study Discussion Questions ———————

What one thing most stood out to you in your Bible study this past week?

Of what did Satan accuse Job in Job 1:10?

Regarding God's hedge of protection around Job and possibly around us: What suggests to you that God has protected you at times in your life?

What evidence suggests that God has allowed gaps in your hedge of protection?

Why do you suppose some people seem to enjoy trafficking in others' misery? How have you learned to deal with "crepe hangers"?

Does the inability to determine the source or blame for suffering complicate your ability to deal with hurts? If so, how?

Regarding Job's stoic response to all his losses, 'Should we accept only good from God and not adversity?' Throughout all this Job did not sin in what he said" (Job 2:10), respond to the questions below.

What do you think was particularly good, godly, or healthy about Job's response?

Do you think anything in Job's response might have been lacking or unhealthy? If so, what?

How do you compare how Job dealt with his grief to how Jeremiah responded to his (see Jeremiah 10:19-20; 12:1-4)?

Notes

Week 3: Personal Bible Study
Satan's Second Test: Job 2:1-10

A friend sent me an anonymous quote that ministers to me as I've dealt with my own journey through grief: "Grief never ends but it changes. It's a passage, not a place to stay. Grief is not a sign of weakness, nor a lack of faith. It's the price of love."

Think of a major loss you suffered at least a few years ago. How is the grief still with you?

How has the grief changed with time?

What does the idea that grief is the price of love mean to you?

This week we'll examine more of Job's journey through grief. His grief over his children is about to be complicated by further attacks on his body.

You'd think that all Satan did to Job in chapter 1 would be enough, but once again Satan appears in God's court. Again God points to Job's faithfulness. He has maintained his integrity even in the face of the calamities crashing down on him.

> Then the Lord said to Satan, "Have you considered My servant Job? No one else on earth is like him, a man of perfect integrity, who fears God and turns away from evil. He still retains his integrity, even though you incited Me against him, to destroy him without just cause."
> "Skin for skin!" Satan answered the Lord. "A man will give up everything he owns in exchange for his life. But stretch out Your hand and strike his flesh and bones, and he will surely curse You to Your face."
> "Very well," the Lord told Satan, "he is in your power; only spare his life." So Satan left the Lord's presence and infected Job with terrible boils from the sole of his foot to the top of his head. Then Job took a piece of broken pottery to scrape himself while he sat among the ashes (Job 2:3-8).

Job 2:3 presents one of those concepts we simply can't easily absorb. It says Satan "incited" God against Job "to destroy him without just cause." If we take that as the complete picture, then we'd understand the Bible to say God was unjust. In fact many in our world do accuse God of injustice.

How do you deal with the accusation that God is unjust?

Luke 22:31 provides an additional piece of the puzzle. What did Satan ask to do to Simon Peter?

What good do you think could come from Peter being sifted?

I confess I don't understand in Job how Satan, a created being, could goad God into anything. I certainly don't know how the idea can fit into our lives today. Does God allow Satan to harm God's children? The implication is too horrible to contemplate, but possibly the idea of Satan sifting Peter explains something of life as we know it.

I don't think this refers to sifting flour to make a pie crust. I think sifting through the litter box to get the chunks out of the kitty litter would be more the idea. I certainly understand that we have things in our lives that need to be removed. So to see that God uses Satan to sift out those parts of our lives really isn't a pleasant thought, but it does make sense to me.

Think back in your life experience. Can you describe how God used something painful to sift something out of your life that needed to go? Consider sharing your experience with the group this week.

How has God changed you for the better through suffering that seemed completely wrong at the time?

If you struggle with that question, consider Psalm 73. The psalmist confessed the envy that threatened to take over his life:

> *But as for me, I almost lost my footing.*
>   *My feet were slipping, and I was almost gone.*
> *For I envied the proud*
>   *when I saw them prosper despite their wickedness*
> *(Psalm 73:2-3, NLT).*

When have you struggled with the issue the psalm writer raised? How does the apparent unfairness of evil people succeeding strike you?

Which side of the issue seems most troubling: good people suffering or bad people prospering? Why?

If you carefully read the rest of Psalm 73, you find that God used the difficulty in the psalmist's life. He asked himself if he had been foolish by trying to follow God's righteousness (v. 13). But the difficulties eventually drove the psalmist to seek God and gain His perspective:

> So I tried to understand why the wicked prosper.
>   But what a difficult task it is!
> Then I went into your sanctuary, O God,
>   and I finally understood the destiny of the wicked
> (Psalm 73:16-17, NLT).

The psalmist struggled with what philosophers call the problem of evil. Many people have abandoned faith in God because they could not reconcile God's goodness with the evil in the world. The psalmist didn't answer the question, but he did something better. He allowed the suffering to draw him to God rather than push him away.

> Then I realized that my heart was bitter,
>   and I was all torn up inside.
> I was so foolish and ignorant—
>   I must have seemed like a senseless animal to you.
> Yet I still belong to you;
>   you hold my right hand.
> You guide me with your counsel,
>   leading me to a glorious destiny.
> Whom have I in heaven but you?
>   I desire you more than anything on earth (Psalm 73:21-25, NLT),

The Bible clearly teaches that God is entirely good, yet He allows the most extreme evil to fall on His children. We can't always see the purpose of such suffering, but sometimes we can.

How greatly would you say that the problem of evil has impacted your thinking and your faith?

Please don't jump to simplistic answers. One way of looking at the entire Book of Job is that God gave it to help us wrestle with the problem of evil.

We want clear-cut answers, especially when we are hurting. The idea that God would allow Satan to toy with us can feel like we're adrift in a tiny lifeboat in a stormy sea. We'll come back to the question of evil again. By the time we get to the end of Job we will see some truths that, while not simple, can minister to our souls.

We'll see that though God clearly allows evil to impact us, He never stops loving us. God's purpose is not only bigger than the evil we face; God's purpose even uses the evil to bring good in our lives.

Randy Alcorn makes a tremendous point in his book Heaven. Many Christians believe that we will have a type of amnesia in Heaven. They think we will be unable to remember our loved ones who are not there because we could not be happy if we knew our lost loved ones' fate. Randy argues that God has no amnesia, and He is the happiest being in the universe. What we will have in Heaven is perspective. We will see all of life from God's perfect view, so we'll know and agree that all God has done is right.

The Book of Job aims at a similar perspective. God is so clearly good that He needs no public relations department. We don't need to polish God's image or defend Him. If we'll stick with the story, then we'll see in the end that God was bringing about the best for Job from the beginning—even when appearances make that seem impossible. Look for a moment at the next passage in the book.

> "Skin for skin!" Satan answered the LORD. "A man will give up everything he owns in exchange for his life. But stretch out Your hand and strike his flesh and bones, and he will surely curse You to Your face."
> "Very well," the LORD told Satan, "he is in your power; only spare his life." So Satan left the LORD's presence and infected Job with terrible boils from the sole of his foot to the top of his head. Then Job took a piece of broken pottery to scrape himself while he sat among the ashes (Job 2:4-8).

What argument did Satan make in Job 2:4-5?

What additional permission did God grant to Satan and what restriction did God place on Satan (v. 6)?

In what condition did that leave Job (vv. 7-8)?

So now the body of the Book of Job really begins. He has lost his children, his wealth, and his health. Job is left alone with his grieving and angry wife who bids him "curse God and die" (v. 9). She can see no other recourse for the situation.

That cheery bit of advice helps me feel connected to Job, because I too have heard that advice—just in different words. The fact that I've not taken the advice is testimony to the Holy Spirit's fortitude in my life. When I read Job and I see that every time he had a moment to just throw up his hands and quit, he hung in there. He didn't give in to discouragement; even when he would lay in pain and in silence, he still didn't curse God. He just laid in silence.

I've been there, and although I wouldn't curse God, I sure didn't want to move, talk, or be. I've been in that dark place where I just did not want to face the day anymore. Let me just let minutes tick by. Let me just get one hour behind me. Yes, I have been that broken before and sad before.

How about you? What has put you in the spot where though you weren't going to curse God and die, you could only lay there?

So these things we've read introduce us to Job and his story. What follows in the book are three series of speeches by Job's friends and his replies to them. The three friends seem to share a single viewpoint and purpose. They aim to convince Job that all his suffering is his fault. If Job would only confess his secret sin, God's blessing would once again appear in his life. The three friends are followed by a young and self-important hot head with a similar goal. Finally, at the end of the book we'll hear God's perspective.

Before we move from the set up of the book in chapters 1 and 2, Job would make one more amazing declaration of faith. Job questioned his wife, "Should we accept only good from God and not adversity?" (Job 2:10).

The question is profound. Yes, we must take both the good and the bad in life. Yes, we must recognize God's hand in all things—even when we cannot understand it. But once we answer the question the pain remains. So we must still deal with the losses, grief, pain, depression, and anxiety that crash upon our shores.

In the rest of the Book of Job, we'll see that making a genuine and magnificent faith declaration does not equal bearing up under the crushing hours, days, and weeks to follow. Job's journey has only just begun.

Review and Reflection

As we conclude the setup of the Book of Job, ask yourself these questions and journal your thoughts.

What most impresses you about this man Job?

What most troubles you about Job's situation?

What insight have you gained from this portion of Bible study?

If you're currently in a place where you just want to lay there and can't move, I encourage you to reach out for help. Find a pastor or Christian counselor who can help you share how you feel. Don't wait. Please, do it today!

BRANCHES
RECOVERING HOPE   RESTORING LIVES
counseling center

www.BranchesCounselingCenter.com
(615) 904-7170

Notes

Week 4: Group Time

Doubt

The discussion topic for this week is doubt, a side effect of loss and grief, or perhaps a companion to the grief process. The Bible study content comes from Job 2:11–3:26.

Suggested Opening Prayer: Heavenly Father, when we hurt, we begin to question, and often we look for someone to blame. Thank You that You are the source of all truth and are not threatened by our questions. Thank You also that You use our doubt to chip away at the false beliefs and assumptions in our lives as well. We ask that this week You would make us honest in our doubt. Teach us to come to You with our questions rather than allowing them to drive us from Your presence. In Jesus' name we pray, amen.

Movie Clip

As a group, watch the Bible Study-Week 4 video clips from the Laughing In The Dark DVD. You will find them on the special features section of the disc.

Video Discussion Questions

How has grief contributed to doubting yourself, your past actions, and decisions?

How do grief and doubt lead to feelings of jealousy toward other people?

What kinds of circumstances contribute to your feelings of being alone?

What actions by friends or family members help you most when dealing with doubt and aloneness?

Would you say you tend more to doubt yourself, to doubt God, or both? Why do you think that's your tendency?

Bible Study Discussion Questions ———————

What one thing most stood out to you in your Bible study this past week?

Think of a major loss you suffered at least a few years ago. How is the grief still with you?

How has the grief changed with time?

What does the idea that grief is the price of love mean to you?

How do you deal with the accusation that God is unjust?

Can you describe how God used something painful to sift something out of your life that needed to go?

How has God changed you for the better through suffering that seemed completely wrong at the time?

How have you struggled with the unfairness of seeing evil people prosper while others suffer?

Week 4: Personal Bible Study
Helpful Friends: Job 2:11-3:26

Psychologists use the term grief work. Grieving really is work—very hard work. Like all other forms of work, we can procrastinate dealing with it, and when we do, it usually just builds up. Also like other kinds of work, we do grief work better when we do it with help. When we are hurting we desperately need friends. Sometimes we may not WANT them, but we need them.

Job was not only a remarkable man in himself; he also had some remarkable friends.

Now when Job's three friends—Eliphaz [EL ih faz] the Temanite, Bildad [BIL dad] the Shuhite, and Zophar [ZOH fahr] the Naamathite—heard about all this adversity that had happened to him, each of them came from his home. They met together to go and sympathize with him and comfort him. When they looked from a distance, they could barely recognize him. They wept aloud, and each man tore his robe and threw dust into the air and on his head. Then they sat on the ground with him seven days and nights, but no one spoke a word to him because they saw that his suffering was very intense (Job 2:11-13).

What evidences do you find in the verses above that show Eliphaz, Bildad, and Zophar were true friends?

Various people have taught seminars and written books on how to be a friend to someone who is hurting. These three friends could have taught the seminar—at least for the first week. They lived out really good guidelines for helping grieving friends.

1. They met together. Most undertakings of any real importance are bigger than one person. We need each other. Give Job's three friends a plus for joining forces to care for their friend.

2. They went. Simple, but essential. They got up off the couch and went. Good intentions really don't count for much. They also didn't send a text or an email.

3. They went to sympathize with and comfort Job. It didn't go well, but at least they went for the purpose of mourning with their friend.

4. They looked. They observed. Admittedly Job's condition was so extreme they hardly could have missed it, so they may have gotten limited credit for this one. But when you consider how we often get wrapped up in ourselves, our own pain, or our own agendas, the fact that they looked and saw certainly deserves mention.

5. They wept. They did all the things appropriate in ancient culture to show extreme grief. Sometimes nothing means as much as someone who'll just cry with you.

6. They sat, silently, for seven days, keeping their opinions to themselves. Amazing.

Review the actions of the three friends. Which one or ones do you think are most important?

When you are hurting, which actions minister most to you?

Can you think of anything they did wrong at this point or that they should have done differently? Explain your response.

Which of the actions do you find most difficult when you seek to care for a hurting friend? Why do you think that's the case?

Because of subsequent events the phrase "Job's friends" has come to mean bad friends who blame the victim. In all fairness we ought to recognize they didn't start out that way. Eventually, Job's friends showed an extraordinary level of compassion. When we're seeking to be good friends we need to recognize what happened and how it went wrong.

I am blessed to say that I have had friends that still weep with me about my sisters. They passed away in the late 1970's, and to this day my friend Julie and I will sometimes just sit and have a good cry, all the while laughing and celebrating the memories of my sisters. I have also had to deal with those "Job's friends" who allowed their own impatience or dysfunction to heap judgment or pain until it simply made things worse in my life.

Grief dramatically changes us. It affects how we react to things we could otherwise deal with effectively. It alters our temperament. It changes how we relate to others.

___

Have you seen out-of-character actions in yourself or others during times of grief? If so, how?

___

Hurting people do a variety of destructive things. When we're hurting we tend to strike out at those around us. We sometimes vent in ways we wouldn't if we were not in pain. So it was with Job. He began to say some rash and questionable things.

In my Bible the heading for chapter 3 is "Job's Opening Speech." Job began to vent his feelings by cursing the day of his own birth. Job understandably wished he had never been born.

> *May the day I was born perish,*
> *and the night when they said,*
> *"A boy is conceived."*
> *If only that day had turned to darkness!*
> *May God above not care about it,*
> *or light shine on it (Job 3:3-4).*

Eliphaz, Bildad, and Zophar just couldn't control themselves. They took the bait and had to correct Job. Instead of simply letting him vent, they went on the attack. The three had been such good friends.

They'd done all the right things. But in joining Job's argument they undermined their own efforts to encourage him. They also demonstrated the basic idea behind their worldview: bad fortune meant that God had to be punishing the person.

Do you identify in any way with the three friends so far? If so, how?

Have you "taken the bait" and argued with someone when you later realized you'd have done better to simply listen? If so, what happened?

Why do you think we have such a strong drive to speak when we'd be better letting it be?

Ecclesiastes 5:2 counsels us, "do not be hasty to speak, and do not be impulsive to make a speech before God. God is in heaven and you are on earth, so let your words be few." Now that's some sound advice that we mostly avoid, isn't it?

I'll add a bit of my own observation: Be really slow to give advice. Even if the advice is on target—at least from our own perspective—it can sometimes have a negative effect. It can say to the other person, "I'm smarter than you. I know better how to run your life than you do." Advice can often feel like a subtle put down. It might be better to leave it to the professionals.

Even if we happen to be right and they happen to take our advice, in the process we might have undermined our friend. We might be affirming the idea that he or she isn't capable or competent. Is that really the message we want to send?

Generally, what can you do rather than give advice?

Instead of giving advice, try what Dr. John Drakeford called modeling the role. Modeling the role is taking the lead to be vulnerable to the other person. If you think they need to open up and be vulnerable, you go first. We can never fully understand someone the way God does. What you can do is share a bit of your own struggle, confess a bit of your own failure, and then be silent. You've given the other person a chance to talk if they wish, but you've left the decision up to them.

When you're grieving and someone begins to give you advice, how do you feel?

Now instead, how would you feel if they said something like, "I can't imagine how you feel. I feel so alone when something like this happens to me?" And then they just let you respond or not, but they didn't say anything more.

Would a person sharing a bit of vulnerability like that be better than advice? Why or why not?

Here I am giving advice about not giving advice, but bear with me a little longer. What helps me is when a friend simply opens the door to conversation. If I want to go through it, I do. They don't try to be the hero and tell me how they solved the problem. They don't put me on the spot with a question.

I have a group of girlfriends I have remained close to since high school (that's a long time): Meribeth, Kim, Patrice, Mary, Gina, and Necy. When possible, we all (or at least some) try and get together once a year. Many of those years I have been smack in the middle of my grief. The greatest things they have done for me then was just BE. It sounds like a miracle, but it is possible for six women to just sit in a room and talk about nothing!

What do you think Job's friends could have said better in response to Job's depressed tirade?

Just for fun, what would have been three really bad things to say? Plan to discuss those with your group this week. We like to have fun together, right?

As my career has progressed, I have revealed pieces of my story to the world, mainly as the healing and revelation came to me. Then a time came when all of the pain and what I was going through became so public, that if I don't talk about it, I would really look crazy. That's how it's been with me as time has gone on.

When I first started sharing my story, I had lost both sisters and my parents were divorced. Those three little statements were, at the time, my entire testimony. Then I realized the impact that my sharing was making when people would say, "Wow, my sister died when I was in high school. Thank you for verbalizing that. No one ever has." So I started thinking, wow, I should tell more stories about Charlotta and Cheralyn. The audience is relating to that.

People always laugh and say, "I appreciate your honesty." I think we even have people in the movie thanking me for being so vulnerable. I thought, I don't know if I'm being vulnerable or if I just need to talk to somebody.

In an odd way, I relate to Job; he lost oxen and donkeys. Then he lost servants. Then a lightning storm burned up his sheep, and he lost his farm. Then all of a sudden his house collapsed, and he lost his kids. The events became so big that they became a story. First, it was just a fluke. Then the next was really bad timing. But when the sheep were all burned up, a pattern of unlucky years was forming. Then it became so obvious that Job's difficulties weren't just unlucky—it was clearly spiritual warfare.

Job refused the temptation to curse God, and instead he cursed the day of his own birth. Many of us who have battled chronic pain can identify with Job on that one.

Have you dealt with something so draining and painful for so long that never being born seemed appealing? If so, what does the chronic struggle do over time?

If you don't identify personally, think of Job. What did the persistent loss and pain do to a man who was so strong? Why?

Finally in this first outburst from Job, notice his statement, "For the thing I feared has overtaken me, and what I dreaded has happened to me" (Job 3:25).

Read Job 1:5. What does Job's fear suggest to you about his practice of constantly offering sacrifices for his grown children?

I'd say all the loss wasn't the beginning of Job's fear. He had lived with fear all along. He couldn't be an objective parent because of his fear. Isn't it ironic that when we let fear take over our lives, it often contributes to the very thing we feared in the first place? Maybe that's part of what the saying "fear is praying to the wrong god" is all about.

So we go from loss to grief to doubt. I have an odd opinion about doubt. To me, doubt is a good thing. Now to stay in doubt can become destructive. However, God often uses doubt to get our attention. So if you let doubt be a catalyst to find an answer, you'll find it. I always tell people, the Word of God has the answer to everything. You might not like it, and the answer might be no, but it will lead to something.

I've learned to embrace my doubt and be OK with it. Sometimes we have a time of doubt and we immediately throw up our hands and say, I'm just not the spiritual Christian I thought I was. I'm going to hell. If you grew up in a Holiness church like I did, you're going to go to hell in a handbasket if you doubt while walking across the room.

How do you deal with times of doubt?

○ I just don't let myself doubt.
○ I get really depressed.
○ I turn to study to resolve my doubt.
○ I talk to a friend or mentor about my doubt.
○ Other _____

What have you learned that has helped most with times of doubt?

It's hard to get into this theological discussion. Many times women have said to me, "I just have such doubt that God is with me, or I'm doubting that God loves me." What I say to those women is this: "Good, as long as you have doubt, you've got something." In my opinion, it's the one who has no doubt and has decided God is dead who really has a problem.

Doubt means you've still got some entanglement of relationship. When you choose to embrace the doubt, you're moving in the right direction. Embracing the struggle is good; however, running from it won't help you get through the adversity. But if you have doubt, that means you're going to go searching for an answer. And God says if you seek Him, you will find Him (see Jeremiah 29:13).

If we're not careful, then we give those pat churchy answers for someone in doubt. We say they have weak faith or that doubting is a sin, but it isn't. A Spanish philosopher named Miguel de Unamuno once said, "Faith which does not doubt is dead faith." Doubt is OK. Doubt is not a sin. It's a catalyst.

You see, I have a lot of confidence in God. Doubt can be the first nudge to point us to the truth: we need each other. We need a friend. In Job's case, sitting in the ash heap, scraping his sores, with losses far too great to bear alone, he desperately needed the support of friends.

I hope this portion of study has been helpful. Being a good friend isn't easy. We need to develop the skills to minister to each other without cutting people to pieces.

Review the section on how to be a friend. What skills help to be a really good friend? Make a list to share with your group.

Now make an opposite list of things to do to be a really bad friend.

It's important to note Job needed a different friend than that wife of his. This just struck me as funny… when all the livestock and riches were gone, the only one left was a wife. For some reason, I don't know why I found that funny because my husband would say the first one who needed to go was that wife. "Give me back an ox and two sheep, Lord, and I'll let you take the wife." No, that's probably not a good idea.

Job lost everything but his wife, and she seemed like one huge hot mess. All she had to say to Job was, "'Do you still retain your integrity? Curse God and die!'" (Job 2:9). Now that would make a good Hallmark card, wouldn't it?

In closing this week's study, I have to warn you. Things are about to go from agonizing to worse. All the way from chapter 4 to chapter 38 the Book of Job gives us a series of arguments. One at a time, Job's three friends speak, and speak, and speak. Their messages each came down to one directive: "You did it. What was it? Confess, 'cause it's your fault." In each case Job responded with, "I did not." Then they do the whole thing over again, "Did too." "Did not!" "Did too!"

So here's the good news. We're not going to spend a week on every "did too" or "did not." We'll look at Eliphaz's first lecture. Then we're going to jump to God's response to all of them.

Review and Reflection

So far, what do you most admire about Job.

What do you admire about his friends?

What do you think Job's friends could have done to keep their relationship with Job from going so wrong?

What do you see from this section of Job that you can apply to your life circumstances?

Week 5: Group Time

Truth

Unlike our other weekly topics, our use of truth requires a bit more explanation. Throughout the body of the Book of Job, God allowed Job's friends to hurl accusations his way. In the process, God permitted Job and his friends to exhaust themselves before He revealed Himself. And by truth, I mean the process of finally coming to the end of ourselves so we turn to God. We usually only find truth when we finally cease struggling with our own answers so we can accept God's. The Bible study content comes from Eliphaz's first speech in chapters 4–5.

Suggested Opening Prayer: Heavenly Father, thank You that Jesus is the truth Who will make us free. Thank You that You use even the wrong in our world to drive us to the One who is right. We confess that we have lived in and followed falsehood. We recognize that without You we cannot overcome the lies both outside and inside our lives. This week we pray that Your Holy Spirit will use our study of Job and the members of our group to draw us to the Truth. In His name we pray, amen.

Movie Clip

As a group, watch the Bible Study-Week 5 video clips from the Laughing In The Dark DVD. You will find them on the special features section of the disc.

Video Discussion Questions

What kinds of bad advice have you followed, only to find later how lousy it actually was?

How does David's candid story of sliding into alcoholism impact the way you think about addiction?

Chonda blamed herself for not seeing David's addiction. How do you deal with self-recrimination?

When Chonda got an award for being the top selling female comedian in history she said she would trade that award in for a day with her grandson in the park. Can you relate to climbing a ladder only to discover it was leaning on the wrong wall? If so, how?

How do you think God seeks to break through to us in places of dark, deep sadness?

How did the truth of Jesus break through to you?

Bible Study Discussion Questions

What one thing most stood out to you in your Bible study this past week?

What positive things did you notice about Job's three friends? Which actions of the three impressed you most? When you're hurting, which actions minister to you most?

Can you think of anything the three friends initially might have done differently? Explain.

When have you seen out-of-character actions in yourself or others during times of grief?

Why do you think we have such a strong drive to speak when we'd be better letting it be?

When you're grieving and someone begins to give you advice, how does it make you feel?

Why do you think sharing a bit of vulnerability (modeling the role) is better than advice?

What do you think Job's friends could have said better in response to Job's depressed tirade?

Just for fun, what would have been three really bad things to say?

Notes

Week 5: Group Time - Truth

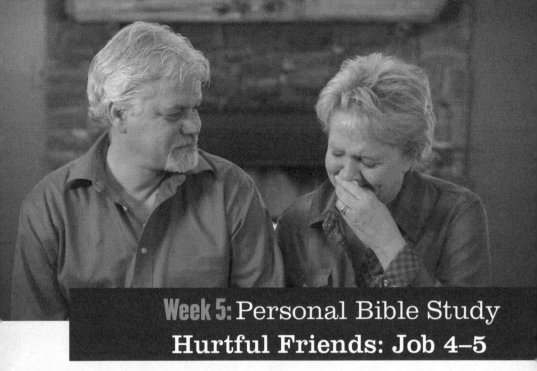

Week 5: Personal Bible Study
Hurtful Friends: Job 4–5

I'm encouraged by the fact that Job had friends who sat with him for seven days. For seven days they just suffered in silence with him. The great thing Job had going for him were no electronics. His friends had to go as human beings in the flesh. We have come to rely on, "Let me just text her and see how she's doing."

What do you sense that we're losing by depending on electronic communications?

One trouble with electronic communication is that we can lie. You can say the word "fine" and everyone will interpret that like nobody's business. Back in Job's day they had a little bit of an advantage. You couldn't call. You had to walk as a human being into that room and say, "How are you doing?"

So often we think a text, an email, or a card is enough. It's not.

Sometimes you just need flesh, bones, and a hug. That was one of the sweet things in Job's story. He had some of those people around. Of course he also had that nagging wife, and the support went wrong when his supporters became critics.

You may have heard the advice to keep your friends close and your enemies closer. The practical truth is that with some friends we really can't tell the difference. Pressure and pain often turns friends into enemies, and so it was with Job's companions. They started out to comfort him but stayed to condemn.

Do you have a story of a friend or friends who became enemies? I can't sit with you and let you tell your story, but I'd like to. Write a bit about the loss as a way to express it.

What wisdom can you gain from reflecting on the story you just considered?

Backhanded Compliments

The 1980s television show The Golden Girls featured a group of senior citizen girlfriends who specialized in backhanded compliments—insults in disguise. Some of my favorites include Blanche saying "Go to sleep sweetheart, pray for brains," and Rose with, "Let's face it, Blanche, you have Bette Davis eyes ... and Freddy Kruger hands!"

We've all heard backhanded compliments: "I love that you'll just wear anything." "Why don't you try to look this cute all the time?" I was sitting on a movie set once when the leading lady in the chair next to me said, "That really is your voice. Wow! You should be in a cartoon!" And I love this one by a little child: "Mommy I like your mustache much better than Daddy's. His is scratchy, but yours is nice and soft."

Job's friends are about to show themselves masters of the subtle and not-so-subtle digs. Listen as Job's first friend, Eliphaz speaks:

> *"Should anyone try to speak with you when you are exhausted? Yet who can keep from speaking?" (Job 4:2).*

I think the translation of that would be, "Job, I've had it. Obviously you are beside yourself and need me to straighten you out."

Hey Eliphaz, here's a hint. When you begin with "who can keep from speaking," that's your own mouth telling you to keep from speaking. I'd say to shut it, but that would be unkind.

Eliphaz continued,

> *Consider: who has perished when he was innocent?*
> *Where have the honest been destroyed?*
> *In my experience, those who plow injustice*
> *and those who sow trouble reap the same (Job 4:7-8).*

From that excerpt, what was the essence of Eliphaz's message?

If you said something like "Job, you are to blame; you brought this on yourself," then I think we're on the same page. Eliphaz somehow thought Job confessing his secret sin would improve the situation.

If you were giving Eliphaz the benefit of the doubt, what good reason might he have for trying to get Job to admit blame?

What other reasons might Eliphaz and his friends have for tearing Job down?

Thinking positively, Eliphaz and company apparently believed that God would forgive and restore if Job confessed his sins. Of course that was based on the false idea that God was punishing Job in the first place. The friends' understanding of God and the universe simply didn't allow for an explanation beyond faulting Job. If something bad has happened, then God must be punishing you. Ouch!

On the other hand, we've all known people who tried to elevate themselves by tearing down others. When the blinders came off of my eyes about one such friend, God allowed me to realize how many times she demeaned others to elevate herself—even to the point of hindering my healing to make herself look needed. So certainly Eliphaz also just could have been trying to one-up Job. Such friends make statements like: "Well, the common denominator in all your problems is you!"

Most, if not all of us, have experienced a time when a good friend turned to blaming when we just needed a listening ear. What do those situations feel like to you?

What would you like to say to your blaming friend?

At such moments I find I want to grab them by the lower lip, pull it over the top of their heads, and say, "Yes, and coincidently this hurts, doesn't it?" I know, I didn't say I'd do it, just that sometimes I want to.

How to Deal with Errant Friends

We can plainly see Job's three friends transition from supportive to condemning. What's more difficult is to figure out what to do about it. Did this mean they were no longer Job's friends? They had proved themselves extremely supportive—to a point. Then they failed miserably. How are we to deal with imperfect friendships and flawed friends?

How do you generally deal with friends who betray a trust or otherwise prove to be flawed?

- ○ It's one and done. I kick 'em to the curb.
- ○ I just try to overlook it and pretend it doesn't hurt.
- ○ I confront them and tell them how they've hurt me.
- ○ I back away and just don't trust them again.
- ○ Other _____

A friend shared a helpful concept called the friendship ladder. Picture yourself and your friend on a ladder. The first rung might be casual acquaintance. The next we'll call common interests. Then comes shared experiences. With every rung of the ladder we increase the intimacy in the friendship.

Here's where the concept proves helpful to me. Different friends occupy different levels of friendship. Some are casual friends with whom you wouldn't think of sharing your most intimate secrets. Some are such close friends that you feel you can trust them no matter what. Very few people, however, are trustworthy enough to occupy the highest steps. Almost everyone you know has a limit to how trustworthy you expect them to be—and you do too.

So this means friendship is not a light switch, either turned on or off.

Healthy friends start at the bottom and slowly become closer over time. The friendship ladder has lots of applications.

How do you handle a new acquaintance who already wants to become top-of-the-ladder intimate?

What do you do with someone who has been a valued friend on steps 1-4 but who then proves untrustworthy on level 5?

Who should be in charge of your relationships, you or your friends? Why?

I don't claim to have all the answers, but here are my responses. To the first question, I'm tempted to just run away. Some people who don't have healthy boundaries want to immediately be best friends. At least recognize that you don't have to share more intimacy than you choose. In answer to the last question, you clearly need to control your own relationships. That doesn't mean controlling other people. It means you choose how vulnerable you will be.

The friend who has been proven untrustworthy can be the most difficult. Job's friends fit this category. They had been really faithful. Seven days of silence is a lot of faithfulness. But then for page after page they attacked Job. Just note that when we get to the end, God is going to prescribe some repentance on their part before fellowship can be restored.

I think the big thing about the relationship ladder is realizing it isn't all on or all off. Everybody has their own level of trustworthiness—from soul sister to radioactive-get-away-from-me. Just because someone can't reach the top rung, I don't need to kick him or her off entirely. We can move to a lower rung and still be friends. However, there are those toxic few who sometimes need to be off your ladder completely.

Waking Up to Truth

The topic of truth this week refers to the process of Job and his friends realizing they all have been wrong. In biblical terms it refers to the process of realizing we are sinners who need God to forgive us and change us. God gave the law in the Old Testament to teach us that we need Jesus. Paul the apostle said it this way: "the law was our schoolmaster to bring us unto Christ, that we might be justified by faith. But after that faith is come, we are no longer under a schoolmaster. For ye are all the children of God by faith in Christ Jesus" (Galatians 3:24-26, KJV).

The apostle Paul used the illustration of the law as a schoolmarm. I think I'd use a slightly different image from back in high school. My best friend Meribeth and I were going to skip chemistry. We dreamed up this great plan. We'll hide in the lockers. We were actually thin enough to sit in those half-sized lockers. We could pull our feet in, and they could shut the door. So we were going to skip class by hiding in the lockers and waiting until it got really quiet in the hallway. Then we were gonna sneak out.

Of course, we were like Houdini squeezing ourselves in there. Meribeth and I thought it was a perfect plan. We got a friend to close the doors. We sat in there and waited, and suddenly I heard Meribeth say, "I can't get my door open!" And I said, "I can't either!" We sat in there scrunched up and in great pain until the next period when the halls began filling up again, and someone came to let us out. Of course, then the teachers and everybody knew we'd been trapped in the lockers the entire chemistry class.

We still laugh about that. As a matter of fact, we recreated a picture of the spectacle with someone attempting to pry us out for the yearbook. We'd been stuck in there. It was awful, but we did make it in the yearbook.

Here's the deep theological question: how does the law do to all of us what those lockers did to Meribeth and me?

It's possible that Job came before the giving of the law, but the principle is the same. We have to hit the bottom before we'll look up. We have to be squeezed into a corner before we'll ask for help. The vast body of the Book of Job (chapters 3–38) is filled with this debate between Job and his friends. That debate wore them all out, sort of like those lockers wore us out.

The only way out of those lockers was to be pried out and face the music. When you really grasp the law of God, you realize that all you can do is throw yourself on the mercy of the court. In all that Job went through, God was squeezing him, preparing him for what was to come.

Next week we'll jump to the climax of the book, but I can pull back the curtain a little now. Job had trusted his own integrity. He had thought he could be good in his own power. All of his misfortunes forced him—like a schoolmaster—to open his eyes and see God.

Do you agree that we have to come to see ourselves as hopeless sinners before we can appreciate what Jesus has done for us? Why or why not?

If you still don't agree, let's go down to the school and look for some lockers. They'll fix you right up—think you'll fit?

I picture what Paul described for us, and what Job experienced, with a distinctly country image. If you go to a ranch that raises cattle, you'll learn about a squeeze chute. It starts with a pen that holds the cattle. The exit from the pen leads to a path that slowly becomes narrower and narrower until only one cow will fit. Then comes the squeeze chute. As each cow enters, the path is closed in front and behind, and the sides of the chute squeeze the cow so she can't move. Then the rancher can administer medication or other treatment needed for the cow's health.

Now speaking of women, the prophet Amos calls the women in his day "cows of Bashan," so I think I'm on solid interpretive ground here. That was Amos 4:1, look it up. Now, don't shoot the messenger—I'm not calling us all cows! And it is perfectly OK to laugh at how the prophet said things as long as you pay attention to what he said.

How do you feel about the image that God herds us into a squeeze chute sometimes because He knows we won't take our medicine on our own?

If the rancher has cows that require treatment, they would have great difficulty catching and subduing each cow for their own good. But the squeeze chute provides what the cows need, even if not what they want or think they need.

How do you think all Job went through, including the abuse by his friends, pushed him down a path to ultimately hear God speak?

At the beginning of the book, Job thought he could handle things on his own. He'd offered up enough sacrifices and had enough integrity. Then Satan came along and tore up all of Job's preconceptions. I think we all need some of that too—without the boils of course.

One of the things I would like to see for us coming out of six weeks of discussion and study of Job would be our shoulders held a little higher. It's one of the reasons that still after 25 years as a stand-up comedian, I still drag myself to the bus. I want you to grasp this truth: God's got this. He's bigger than you or I thought He was. Whatever I'm going through, however deep the hole I seem to be in, God has not forgotten me. He has not forgotten you. He is trustworthy. I think everybody, but especially women, need to get that message.

In all you've gone through, God continues to draw you to Himself. What would that thought mean to you in your journey?

A lot of women have been disappointed by men—that's just the sadness of the world. Many times the first man to disappoint us was our daddy. That means the trust of that covenant relationship has been broken. So it is a long journey for that child to grow up and learn what the fatherhood of God is like.

The same applies with wives and husbands. Husbands, be good to your wives because when you're not, you break that covenant relationship. When that's broken, to trust again is very hard. In our humanness and brokenness, we equate human emotions, like untrustworthiness, to the nature of God. So women, one of my primary purposes of this study is that you will leave thinking, Wait a minute, God is trustworthy.

In so many ways we've all experienced the broken covenant with God. We need to recognize that the primary purpose of the Bible message deals with restoring that covenant.

How do you react to that understanding of Scripture?

I want you to leave this study with a deeper understanding of the trustworthiness of God. When that happens, healing occurs in a lot of other areas. You can let some of the pain go. You can walk out of this thing you've been harboring or this hurt that you can't let go.

That's what people need to know about the Lord. I beat myself up over mistakes I've made and God hasn't even considered them. He's removed them as far as the east is from the west. We're the ones who have trouble letting those things go. I would love to help women move a little ahead in that process.

Review and Reflection

As you review and summarize this week's study, what makes you believe God is trustworthy?

What challenges your sense that you can trust God?

Does God's willingness to squeeze us into the place we need to go make you trust Him more or cause you to struggle more?

Notes

Week 6: Group Time

Grace

The discussion topic for this week is grace, a word not found but definitely displayed in Job. Loss begins the grief process, which leads us to doubt many things. Doubt actually paves the way for truth as we come to question old beliefs. When we have stripped away the false, truth opens the door for grace. The Bible study content for week 6 comes from Job 38–42.

Suggested Opening Prayer: Heavenly Father, we fall before You in gratitude for Your grace. You have given us Your riches at Your Son's expense. You have extended to us forgiveness and accompanied it by Your Spirit. We pray that, like the pure in heart and our friend Job, we would see God. This week humble us like you did the ancient patriarch. Teach us to turn from self-centeredness to Christ-centeredness. Reveal Yourself to us we pray, in Jesus' name, amen.

Movie Clip

As a group, watch the Bible Study-Week 6 video clips from the Laughing In The Dark DVD. You will find them on the special features section of the disc.

Video Discussion Questions

Psalm 37:4 says: "Take delight in the LORD, and He will give you your heart's desires." How does taking delight in the Lord fit into His fulfilling your heart's desires?

How has God given you your heart's desires? How has he not?

How does Psalm 37:1-2 fit the story of Job?

For you, what does it mean that Jesus is the answer?

We know Jesus will one day make all things new, but how does He make things new for you now?

Bible Study Discussion Questions

What one thing most stood out to you in your Bible study this week?

Do you have a story (that you would be able to share without dishonoring anyone) of a friend or friends who became enemies? If so, what do you learn from it?

What good reason do you see for Job's friends treating him as they did?

What less than admirable reason do you see for the four critics' message?

If you have experienced a friend going from supportive to blaming, how did that make you feel?

Why do you think we sometimes turn from listening to either blaming or fixing?

What's your first instinctive reaction when a friend proves untrustworthy?

How does the law accomplish the same thing that Meribeth and I experienced in those high school lockers?

Do you think we have to come to see ourselves as hopeless sinners before we can appreciate what Jesus has done for us? Why or why not?

How do you think that all Job went through, including the abuse by his friends, pushed him down a path to ultimately hear God speak?

What does the thought that God continues to draw you to Himself mean to you in your journey?

What makes you believe God is trustworthy?

What challenges your sense that you can trust God?

--------------------- **Notes** ---------------------

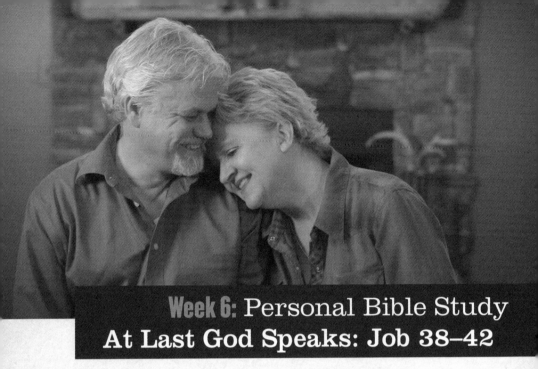

Week 6: Personal Bible Study
At Last God Speaks: Job 38–42

As we've seen before, the Book of Job shares some common themes with the Book of Jeremiah. Both men knew suffering. Jeremiah's call included the concept we are exploring this week in Bible study.

> *See, I have appointed you today*
> *over nations and kingdoms*
> *to uproot and tear down,*
> *to destroy and demolish,*
> *to build and plant (Jeremiah 1:10).*

Jeremiah's ultimate calling was to build and plant, but to reach that calling he would have to uproot and tear down. In our brief survey of Job we've seen how suffering tore down and uprooted Job's comfortable life. Satan's attack on Job stripped away old assumptions and prepared him to see God in a new light.

Can you relate on a practical level? How has suffering in your life made it possible to see God in a clearer way?

We are coming to the conclusion of the Book of Job. Job doesn't use the New Testament term grace, but the concept applies. So much of Job's story involved his dealing with grief and loss. In her book, On Grief and Grieving, Elisabeth Kübler-Ross describes the end of the grieving process as acceptance. It's at that stage we come to a new reality following loss.

What does grace mean to you in regard to the losses you have suffered?

Grace includes adjustment to our new normal, but it involves so much more. Grace means God has entered our reality with forgiveness and restoration through His divine power. Grace is the thing that helps when everything else has been wrong. When all your opinions and all your answers fail the test, grace brings a new start. Grace says "I still love you. Get back on the horse."

Grace also includes hope—grace and hope—we can't have one without the other. Hope is this wonderful entity we're trying to attain. Grace is the vehicle that gets us there. Grace is the thing that keeps me from taking myself so seriously. It's been the greatest gift. And it's not that it gives me the license to just go goof up. I don't want to goof up. (I have such fancy theological terms!)

Grace gives me the awareness that when I do fail, God will be there to give me a second chance—and a third, fourth, and fifth chance. To me, grace is the icing on the cake from the cross. The cross gave us forgiveness and then the cross gave us this extension of forgiveness. The cross gave us the car. Grace gave us the gas.

How does God's grace give you the energy to go on when your power has failed?

Grace got Job through, but it didn't give him his kids back. Without grace, what a miserable end Job's story would have. God gave him so much back, but some things just can't be replaced. Even in the middle of his pain and suffering, God extended grace to Job. This is a great lesson for me. God has been so gracious to me. Out of the abundance of the grace God has shown me, I need to extend grace to others.

For example, I have forgiven my father, but I think it's an unsafe and unhealthy relationship for me to pursue. So far, he has never extended grace, forgiveness, or acknowledged that he did anything wrong. But that's his responsibility, not mine.

What I have done is acknowledge gratitude that my father was a part of bringing me into this world. I honor him through my gratefulness for his role in my birth. Honoring him means I don't plaster his name in every book. Grace means I leave it be. I let it go, even when my brother Mike and I don't see eye-to-eye on that topic or countless others! We are at peace knowing that we are exactly where God has placed us to be in our journey. See, grace states Mike's OK, and I'm OK.

The Conclusion of Job

Now we come to the climactic last five chapters of Job. God stood by as Satan attacked Job's wealth, his family, and his body. God listened as Job sparred with his three friends who wanted Job to accept blame for his own suffering. God even continued to hold His peace as the young hothead, Elihu (ih LEE who), built his simplistic case. Now at last, God would speak to Job:

> *Who is this who obscures My counsel*
> *with ignorant words?*
> *Get ready to answer Me like a man;*
> *when I question you, you will inform Me.*
> *Where were you when I established the earth?*
> *Tell Me, if you have understanding (Job 38:2-4).*

For the next two chapters God schools Job in nature and science. God batters him with a relentless series of questions, each one with the same answer; God knows and Job does not. Finally Job responds:

I am so insignificant. How can I answer You?
I place my hand over my mouth.
I have spoken once, and I will not reply;
twice, but now I can add nothing (Job 40:4-5).

In your experience, how much does it generally take for people to finally shut up and listen?

How about you? How long does the same process take for you?

After further examples of the greatness of God's creation, Job concedes:

Surely I spoke about things I did not understand,
things too wonderful for me to know. …
I had heard rumors about You,
but now my eyes have seen You.
Therefore I take back my words
and repent in dust and ashes (Job 42:3,5-6).

Now that Job sees God, how do you think Job's declaration changes his situation?

Job's vision of God really constitutes the climax of the story. I believe Job was saying: "I formerly thought I was a good man and that my integrity made me right with God. Now I see that compared to God's majesty, I am nothing. I fall on my face and ask God's forgiveness."

Though Job's confession came at a time without the temple, law, or priests, I believe it compares to Isaiah's declaration when he saw the Lord high and lifted up.

> *Then I said:*
> *Woe is me for I am ruined*
> *because I am a man of unclean lips*
> *and live among a people of unclean lips,*
> *and because my eyes have seen the King,*
> *the LORD of Hosts (Isaiah 6:5).*

After Job's confession, the book ends with an epilogue. The divine writer gathers up the pieces of the story, and God deals with them one by one. First came Eliphaz, Bildad, Zophar, and Elihu. God prescribes a unique-in-Scripture solution for them. Normally sacrifice is to be offered only to God Himself, but they are to take seven bulls and seven rams, go to Job and offer a burnt offering for themselves. Then Job is to pray for them, and they will escape God dealing with them as they deserve.

Stop for a moment and think of those who have plagued you. We all have them—people who in small and sometimes large ways have opposed, undermined, or slandered us.

How do you think it felt when God made Job's opponents come to him, offer sacrifices, and request that he pray for them?

How do you think you would feel under similar circumstances?

Finally we come to the last act of this drama. God restored Job and doubled his possessions. God gave Job seven sons and three daughters, and he lived for 140 more years. Job "saw his children and their children to the fourth generation. Then Job died, old and full of days" (Job 42:16-17).

I confess that here I have one of my biggest problems understanding the Book of Job. He got his riches back. OK, you can restore riches. The same for Job's health, it was restored. Apparently Job's wife was still around, because the children had to come from somewhere. But the children? You don't replace dead children. Anybody who's lost a child knows that.

In the case of Job, if God had replaced his kids, then this would indeed be a very difficult story for the rest of us who didn't get our loved ones replaced. Perhaps God looked down through the expanse of time and thought, "I can't give him his kids back because there are going to be millions who never get their kids back, their cancer healed, their finances restored. They will need this story."

Maybe that has something to do with why we picked Job for this study. When we considered it, I thought, I always think of it as a man's story. I don't know why. It never seemed like a feminine story for women to relate to. I've always thought, Ugh, Job. Who wants to talk about Job? But in the course of preparing this study I've come to relate to Job in many ways.

I deeply hope that you have gained some encouragement and strength from our journey through Job together. I hope he feels more like a friend. Most of all, I pray that Job's God has ministered to you. As we conclude, let me ask some final questions to try to gather up the insights we learned from our journey.

Review and Reflection

How has your view of Job, the man, changed through these weeks together?

What does the Book of Job say to you about the problem of human evil and suffering?

What questions does the book still leave unanswered?

Most of all, how does the coming of Jesus help with the questions Job leaves behind?

Notes

Leader's Help

Thank you for considering leading a small group study based on Laughing in the Dark and the Book of Job. We have created this resource to be flexible so you can follow the Holy Spirit's leadership for a small-group experience. Here are some suggestions for starting your Bible study group and some ideas for ways to lead.

Beginning a Bible Study Group

You can use a variety of methods to assemble a group of women for this Bible study. Work with your church leadership to schedule the Laughing in the Dark movie, and then follow up with the study. Or you might invite friends or neighbors to a home viewing and follow with the Bible study. Your church outreach ministry might use the study as a way to minister to your community.

Your group can be as simple as meeting with a couple of friends or neighbors. However, if you want to extend the ministry, enlist others in preparing for your study. The group will be much stronger if several members feel a sense of ownership in the study. You might enlist an overall coordinator, someone to promote the study, a prayer team, people in charge of refreshments, and a team to provide facilities. By sharing the preparation you will have a team who will care about the ministry, and you will not burn out a sole leader.

Make sure that your preparation includes a place to meet (or multiple places in case of more than one group), plans for getting books to group members, refreshments, and leaders for groups.

We have sought to make the group leader plan extremely simple. Get together each week, watch the clips from the DVD, and discuss the questions on the group pages. We've provided many questions to choose from, so don't feel pressure to discuss them all. We simply want to free you and the group up to share in a loving environment. Consider simply asking, "What one thing most stood out to you in your Bible study this past week?" Many times the best group learning will result when members simply share their answer to the question.

Week 1: Watch Laughing in the Dark ———————

The purpose of the first group session is to watch the movie together and launch the Bible study. Plan get-acquainted activities appropriate to your group. By all means make the viewing as comfortable and fun as possible. If you enlisted your group for the Bible study, be sure everyone has a book, and encourage them to complete the personal study for week 1 before next week.

If the movie-goers have not committed yet to the Bible study, invite them to participate. If possible you will want to have books on hand for those who choose to participate. You can see how having a team of women preparing for the study will greatly increase enthusiasm and participation.

Explain that Chonda wanted to provide a way so women could follow up the movie with a Bible study and mutual support. The group will be talking together about the topics raised by both Laughing in the Dark and the Book of Job. Make sure that all the women who want to participate have books. Take a few moments to look at the format of this Bible study. Show them that the personal study is not complex or time consuming. With only a few minutes daily or an hour during the week they can complete the assignments.

Show the group pages that begin each week. Explain that they will be watching some short clips from the movie, discussing them, and sharing their thoughts from the previous week's private study. Tell them that they are welcome to the group with little or much preparation. If they wish they can look over the questions on the group pages each week in order to be better prepared to share. Note that the group pages contain many more questions than you will have time to discuss. You will be able to choose those topics and questions you find helpful.

Invite the group to spend personal time studying Job and writing down their thoughts and feelings.

Encourage members to enjoy the time with Job, Job's strange friends, and Chonda. Ask them to write their responses as if they were meeting, laughing, and crying along with Chonda.

Pray together at the end of the group time.

Week 2: Loss

The purpose of this week's meeting and review is to get to know Job and to consider the topic of loss. In the week 1 Bible study we touched on several themes:

1. Concerning Job: Many people have a very idealized view of the man. We want to begin to see and know him as a real person. He was a man of great integrity but who was possibly more concerned with his own righteousness than with God.
2. The topic of loss: We cannot explain why we experience a given loss. What we can recognize is that losses come in every life and are a part of life. Loss does not mean God is punishing us, nor that His love has failed. The exercise about loss in the stages of life is designed to help us grieve our losses as part of our fallen existence.
3. The problem of evil: Job and the topic of loss both point us to the problem of evil. We cannot answer why bad things happen. We can recognize really bad answers (like when someone says "God picked your child for His garden"). The passages from Matthew 5 and 13 point out that God allows both good and evil to those who don't deserve them.

We will never completely answer our questions about loss or the problem of evil. Even if we could, answers aren't what we need anyway. We need to overcome our loneliness. We need company. We need Jesus, and we need each other. So if the discussion in week 2 helps women to feel an increased connection to Job, to Job's God, and to each other, you will have done an excellent job.

Week 3: Grief

The purpose of this week's meeting and review is to move beyond loss to the grief process. Talking with trusted friends is central to grieving well. Chonda's experience and the losses Job experienced invite us to talk about our own losses.

The questions on the group pages are intended to help your members to talk about their losses and gain strength from the group. Encourage group members to simply love each other in their losses. Steer the discussion away from giving advice and attempting to fix others.

The comparison of Job's and Jeremiah's way of dealing with grief may raise questions. Consider how very differently Jeremiah (10:19-25; 12:1-4) or David (Psalm 39; 73) dealt with their grief compared to Job. They complained and confronted God about their losses. Job seems to have wanted to show he could carry them alone.

Remind members this week that the point of the group is to lovingly support one another. A listening ear and a friendly hug are much more important than the correct answers.

Week 4: Doubt

The purpose of this week's meeting and review is to explore doubt in the grieving process. Doubt can be either good or bad. It can bring about constructive or destructive results in a person's life.

Grief and loss often kick the props out from under parts of our lives. We lose things we've depended on, like employment, a loved one, or our own health. The stability we had can disappear. God gave us the grieving process to find the new strength and balance we need.

Doubt can also serve a painful but needed function in our lives. We need to strip away the false gods on which we've depended. Job had been depending on his own integrity. As impressive as Job's righteousness might have been, it can't compare with redemption in Jesus.

The doubt created by loss can be most destructive when it causes us to reject God. More people may have abandoned faith over the problem of evil than any other cause. So again this week the Bible study explores the accusation that God is unjust. As you prepare for this week's group session, remember that people usually need love more than answers.

Week 5: Truth

You might picture the journey to the truth in two parts. One is the truth itself. The other involves removing the obstacles in the way of truth. If you pictured truth as a magnificent vista, the obstacles are the weeds that block the view. Getting the obstacles out of the way is often more painful and time consuming than embracing the truth itself.

In both the Book of Job and our own grief processes, God sometimes has to strip away the obstacles before we see Him. It took Job an enormous amount of struggle to eventually turn from his integrity and to God. So this week the suggested topic refers to the painful process of stripping away those obstacles.

Job's story sheds light on friendship. As we read and meditate on the book we learn how to recognize and be a good friend. We hope your group members are growing in friendship skills. In terms of our two-part treatment of truth, a good friend won't settle for untruth. But a real friend also practices the more difficult skill—patiently helping to pull the weeds that obscure the truth.

Week 6: Grace

This week's meeting and review moves us toward the desired end of the grieving process and of Job's journey toward God. God will ultimately give us the desire of our hearts—especially when our hearts desire Him. God is the ultimate good. The greatest thing He can do for any of us is to give us Himself. So much of life involves God moving us into the spot where we will finally see that He was what we needed all along.

In the review of the week 5 Bible study, we explore his friends once more. Plan to discuss how God was using Job's friends to push him down a path to ultimately see God. God used the friends even though they were pushing in the wrong direction.

Concluding Your Group

You may choose to conclude your group with the discussion for week 6. Members can complete the final portion of Bible study on their own. Or you might plan a celebration for week 7. We've suggested no format because you can design a celebration to fit your group.

For the Bible study portion you might simply ask:

1. What most stood out to you in your Bible study?
2. What stood out for the final week?
3. What stood out for the entire time together?

We who have brought you this Bible study thank you from the bottom of our hearts for the hard work you have put into the Laughing in the Dark Bible study. We pray you have found a personal friendship with a stubborn but marvelous ancient patriarch. We pray that you've found new and closer relationships with women in your Bible study group. And most of all we pray that you've come to love Job's God in a deeper way.

Thank you.

Notes

- Leader's Help